Working Mothers

Understanding Words in Context

Curriculum Consultant: JoAnne Buggey, Ph.D.
College of Education, University of Minnesota

By Bradley Steffens

Greenhaven Press, Inc.
P.O. Box 289009
San Diego, CA 92198-0009

Titles in the opposing viewpoints juniors series:

Smoking

Gun Control

Animal Rights

AIDS

Alcohol

Immigration

Death Penalty

Drugs and Sports

Toxic Wastes

Patriotism

Working Mothers

Poverty

Cover photo: Myers/UNIPHOTO

Library of Congress Cataloging-in-Publication Data

Working mothers : understanding words in context / [edited] by Bradley
Steffens.
       p.   cm. — (Opposing viewpoints juniors)
    Summary: Presents opposing viewpoints on whether mothers should
work outside the home and what effect this employment has on their
families.
    ISBN 0-89908-644-6
    [1. Working mothers.]—United States—Juvenile literature.
[1. Working mothers.]   I. Steffens, Brad, 1956–   II. Series.
HQ759.48.W67 1989
306.874′3—dc20   89-35434
                                                              CIP
                                                               AC

CONTENTS

An Introduction to
Opposing Viewpoints

When people disagree, it is hard to figure out who is right. You may decide one person is right just because the person is your friend or relative. But this is not a very good reason to agree or disagree with someone. It is better if you try to understand why these people disagree. On what main points do they differ? Read or listen to each person's argument carefully. Separate the facts and opinions that each person presents. Finally, decide which argument best matches what you think. This process, examining an argument without emotion, is part of what critical thinking is all about.

This is not easy. Many things make it hard to understand and form opinions. People's values, ages, and experiences all influence the way they think. This is why learning to read and think critically is an invaluable skill. Opposing Viewpoints Juniors books will help

you learn and practice skills to improve your ability to read critically. By reading opposing views on an issue, you will become familiar with methods people use to attempt to convince you that their point of view is right. And you will learn to separate the authors' opinions from the facts they present.

Each Opposing Viewpoints Juniors book focuses on one critical thinking skill that will help you judge the views presented. Some of these skills are telling fact from opinion, recognizing propaganda techniques, and locating and analyzing the main idea. These skills will allow you to examine opposing viewpoints more easily.

Each viewpoint in this book is paraphrased from the original to make it easier to read. The viewpoints are placed in a running debate and are always placed with the pro view first.

Understanding Words in Context

Whenever you read, you may come across words you do not understand. Sometimes, because you do not know a word or words, you will not fully understand what you are reading. One way to avoid this is to interrupt your reading and look up the unfamiliar word in the dictionary. Another way is to examine the unfamiliar word in context. That is, by studying the words, ideas, and attitudes that surround the unfamiliar word, you can often determine its meaning.

In this Opposing Viewpoints Juniors book, you will be asked to determine the meaning of words you do not understand by considering their use in context.

Sometimes a word that has the same meaning as the unfamiliar word will be used in the sentence or in a surrounding sentence. This word will alert the reader to the meaning of the unfamiliar word. An example is:

Many animal species are **endangered** by human activities. Their lives are threatened by people destroying the environment.

The unfamiliar word is **endangered.** The clue is the word *threatened.* The second sentence is an explanation of how people are endangering animals. It is relating the same idea as the first sentence, but it is a little more specific. So, the words threatened and endangered should mean about the same thing. In fact, they do.

Often, the surrounding sentences will not contain a word similar to the unfamiliar word. They may, however, contain ideas that suggest the meaning of the unknown word. An example is:

The United States has many **assets.** It has beautiful scenery, natural resources, generous people, and great wealth.

The meaning of the word **assets** can be determined by studying the ideas around it. Beautiful scenery, natural resources, generous people, and great wealth are all desirable things to have. Therefore, assets must mean things that are desirable to own.

In some cases, words and ideas that have opposite meanings can offer the reader clues about an unfamiliar word. For example:

Seldom will you find a man with more than one wife. Most men are **monogamous.**

The unfamiliar word is **monogamous.** The clue is *more than one wife* in the first sentence. In this case, a contrast between the first and second sentence is used. The author of this sentence is saying, "You do not usually find this, so you do usually find that," or "You do not usually find a man with more than one wife, so you do usually find a man with only one wife." Monogamous, then, must mean "having only one wife."

Sometimes the meanings of unfamiliar words are more difficult to determine. You just have to pay attention to the meaning of the sentence to figure them out. Here is an example:

Pickpockets can be **incapacitated** by cutting off their hands.

To determine what **incapacitated** means, you first have to figure out what cutting off pickpockets' hands would accomplish. It would stop them from picking people's pockets. So incapacitated must mean that a person is unable to do something.

In many cases, you will not be able to determine what a word means by its use in the sentence. You will have to look it up in the dictionary. Consider the following example:

The crowd gathered in the auditorium. I noticed that everyone looked **pensive.** I wondered what was happening.

In this case, the meaning of **pensive** cannot be determined by its use in the sentence or paragraph. There is not enough information. It could mean *anxious, happy, different, sad,* or *ridiculous.* It means *thoughtful.*

In the following viewpoints, several of the words are highlighted. These words might be unfamiliar to you. You should be able to determine the meanings of these highlighted words by studying them in context—that is, by using the surrounding words and ideas to determine the meaning of the word. As you read the material presented in this book, then, stop at the unfamiliar words and see if you can determine their meanings.

Finally, use a dictionary to see how well you have understood the words in context.

We asked two students to give their opinions on the working mothers issue. We asked them to look up some unfamiliar words and use them in sentences. But they had to use these words in such a way that the reader could determine their meanings. Try to figure out the meanings of the words you do not understand by studying them in context. Check your dictionary to see if you are right.

I believe mothers should work.

People like astronaut Sally Ride, Justice Sandra Day O'Connor, and Britain's Prime Minister Margaret Thatcher have already shown that women can perform as well as men in all kinds of jobs. You should pursue the **vocation** that interests you. No one can tell you what career you should choose just because you are male or female.

Raising children is an important job, too. But who says that mothers are the only ones who can do it? Fathers can stay home, too. If the wife makes more money than the husband, she should work full time. Parents should do what is best for the entire family.

Parents can also put their children in day care. That way, both parents can work. This is what most families do. Mothers and fathers are still important to their kids. They eat with them, teach them family values, help them with schoolwork. Besides, day care can be fun.

My mother works, and I think it's great. I don't see her as much as some kids see their mothers. But I still see her a lot. We have more money for clothes and things than we would if she didn't work. You can tell that she likes her profession. I think she would be unhappy if she could not do the kind of work she enjoys.

I do not believe mothers should work.

Children need their mothers to take care of them, especially when they are small. Mothers and their babies have a special relationship. Day care providers take care of children, but they don't love them as the children's mothers do.

Children raised at home have fewer problems in school than children raised in day care do. When moms work, the kids get into trouble. They commit crimes, like stealing. They use or sell drugs. The mom should stay home and the dad should work. This family structure has worked well for thousands of years. We should keep it.

Mothers who work are selfish. They care more about their own happiness than their children's well-being. Mothers work so they and their children can have more things. But children are not **materialistic.** They do not care about owning stuff. They care about being loved.

My mom stays home, and it's great. Running a household is a full-time job. She enjoys it. She is always there for my sister and me. And I know my dad appreciates it. He is becoming more and more successful because he can concentrate on his job. That's good for all of us. On weekends, my family has time to do fun things because Mom has taken care of all the chores during the week.

Cindy and Christi have very different opinions about women and work. Both of them use words you might not understand. But you should be able to discover the meanings of these words by considering their use in context.

Cindy:

You should pursue the *vocation* that interests you. No one can tell you what career you should choose just because you are male or female.

NEW WORD	CLUE WORD OR IDEA	DEFINITION
vocation	career	a chosen occupation, a career

Christi:

Mothers work so they and their children can have more things. But children are not *materialistic*. They do not care about owning stuff. They care about being loved.

NEW WORD	CLUE WORD OR IDEA	DEFINITION
materialistic	care about owning stuff	to care about owning things

Both Cindy and Christi think they are right about working mothers. Which student do you think is right? Why?

As you read the viewpoints in this book, keep a list of the new words you come across. Write down what you think the words mean from the context. Check your definitions against those in a dictionary.

CHAPTER 1

PREFACE: Can Mothers Have Both Work and Family?

From the time children are small, people want to know what they plan to be when they grow up. The longer children go to school, the more important this question becomes. Teachers and counselors help children choose classes that will prepare them for college or a career. Both girls and boys are prepared for the day when they will seek a job.

It has not always been like this. Not very many years ago, girls were not expected to look for work outside the home. Most girls took courses in homemaking. Very few prepared for college. Many got married, had children, and managed the household.

Today, most Americans—men and women alike—have jobs. But some people think this is a mistake. They believe that many of today's problems, including crime and drug abuse, are the result of mothers leaving the home to work. They see homemaking as a very important profession that should be encouraged, as it once was.

The authors of the following viewpoints debate whether it is possible, practical, and satisfying for mothers to both work and raise children. As you read, you may see words you do not understand. Try to determine the meaning of these words by their use in context. Keep a list of words that are new to you.

Mothers can have both work and family

Editor's Note: This viewpoint is paraphrased from an article by Sharon Nelton and Karen Berney. They are senior editors with *Nation's Business,* a monthly magazine published in Washington, D.C. They argue that women are learning how to balance home and work life, and that the benefits of working outweigh the losses. They discuss "trade-offs," or how women must sometimes make compromises that may hurt their work or their families.

Some words that may be unfamiliar are highlighted. Try to discover their meanings from their use in context. Guidelines for some of these words appear in the margins. Other highlighted words will be discussed in the critical thinking skill at the end of the chapter.

In the traditional American family of the 1950s, the father worked and the mother stayed home with the children. Every night, the family ate dinner together.

Children who grew up in the 1950s might have been expected to carry on the tradition. That is what they were taught. But by the 1970s, women were questioning the traditional roles set aside for them. Many decided to pursue full-time careers. When these women did have children, they often hired baby-sitters to watch their children while they worked. Still, many women wanted to do some things the way their mothers used to.

Claudia Marshall is one such woman. When her workday was done, she rushed home to recreate the home of her youth. She made dinner and her family ate together every night. But as her workdays got longer and longer, she decided something had to change. "I took a close look at the dinner **ritual** and decided it had to go," she said. Instead of preparing the regular nightly meal, she had her baby-sitter feed her son before she got home. She and husband, James, ate later.

Every night and *regular* are clues to the meaning of *ritual*. A *ritual* is something that is done regularly.

SALLY FORTH By Greg Howard

Reprinted with special permission of NAS, Inc.

Giving up the family meal is one of many **trade-offs** Marshall has willingly made. Today she is a vice president with a large insurance company. She is raising two children and has been married for thirteen years. She believes that being a mother has helped her be a better manager. She also believes that her work life helps her family life. She does not feel bad about her decision to trade **domestic** life for a career outside the home. "I cannot imagine having done it any other way," she said.

Women who work also face trade-offs in how they handle their time at home. Because their time at home is limited, women must schedule their home life, too. "Women, who are learning to **maximize** their time at the office, must learn to make the most of their time at home," says Linda Albert, a consultant. Mothers need to make plans and organize tasks at home just as they do at work. "After a hard day's work, you want to 'hang loose,'" she says, "but being organized lets you get the most out of life at home."

Marion Fredman, co-owner of Such A Business, a children's store in Oakland, California, agrees that family life needs to be organized. She says she runs her home "with the same **rigidity**" she uses to run her business. She plans when the family can be together, and those plans do not change unless there is an emergency.

The attitudes of women like Marshall and Fredman are becoming common. Most women today prefer careers to full-time motherhood. According to the Department of Labor, most new mothers return to work within a year of giving birth. Studies of female college graduates show that most young women are training for a career they plan to pursue for the rest of their lives.

While the issue of work and family will affect large companies and the government, women are not waiting for **corporations** or the government to act. They are busy finding ways to have a fair shot at "having it all."

Trade-offs appeared in the editor's note to this viewpoint. What does *trade-off* mean?

Outside the home is the opposite of *domestic*. *Domestic* refers to things *inside the home*.

What is the clue to *maximize*? What does *maximize* mean?

What are clues to the meaning of *rigidity*? What does rigidity mean?

Can women have both work and family?

Ms. Nelton and Ms. Berney say women can work and have a family if they are willing to make "trade-offs." Name one trade-off they describe. After reading the viewpoint, do you agree that women can have both work and family? Why or why not?

2 Mothers cannot have both work and family

Editor's Note: This viewpoint is paraphrased from an article by Amy Gage, managing editor of *Minnesota Monthly,* a feature magazine published by Minnesota Public Radio. She does not believe that women can "have it all." That is, she does not think women can successfully juggle a family and a career.

What is a clue to the meaning of *scoff*? What does *scoff* mean?

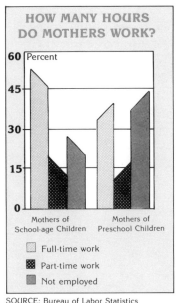

HOW MANY HOURS DO MOTHERS WORK?

Percent

60

45

30

15

0

Mothers of School-age Children   Mothers of Preschool Children

☐ Full-time work

▨ Part-time work

▧ Not employed

SOURCE: Bureau of Labor Statistics

A few years ago, I began to really pay attention to children for the first time since I was a child. I watched them in restaurants, stores, and on the street. I used to **scoff** at the notion of a "maternal instinct," but I do not mock the idea anymore. I think that is what I was experiencing. Sometimes I talked with them. I discovered that I like children, and that they seem to like me. This raised The Question in my mind: Should I have kids, or shouldn't I? What will I give up if I do, and what will I miss if I don't?

A girlfriend and I discussed The Question over breakfast the other day. I have known this woman for many years. She means a lot to me, and I value her opinions. Kitty and her husband will not be having children. She does not believe she would be a good parent. She has no patience with children. She thinks she would demand too much of them.

She also doubted whether she could give a child enough love and affection. "Neither of us had loving parents, so we don't have many **parental** feelings," she said. "It sounds cold-blooded, but it is very expensive to have a child. We would not be able to give a child a lot of material things. Also, we both like what we do for a living. The thought of giving up my job for even three years is very depressing to me."

I was surprised to hear Kitty assume that she would be the parent who would stay home with her children. She and her husband share all of the household tasks. They both value their jobs, and they earn about the same amount of money. Why should she be the one to give up her career?

Actually, I assume the same thing about my own marriage. But why do I believe that I, and not my husband, would be the one who would pay the price for having children? Why do I think that only my career will suffer? I am married to a wise man. He is **enlightened**.

I think the answer is that, deep down, I know that my husband simply cannot take on the **biological** burden. His body cannot carry our child, or give birth, or provide milk. Those are things only a woman can do. Those are tasks that a woman, alone, must face.

I have always wanted to work, to become good at something, and to earn my own money. My mother taught me that having a career was important. Going to college at the height of the women's movement strengthened my belief. To change course now—to have a baby or two and stay home for awhile—would go against everything I have struggled for all these years.

Some women say they can "have it all," but I do not believe it. I have seen many women, including my sisters, try to "have it all." But in the end, something has to give: the marriage, the child's happiness, the father's temper, the mother's career.

And so The Question becomes not "Do I *want* to have children?" but "Should I take the risk?" If other women are not able to have it all, why should I think that I can?

What word provides a clue to the meaning of *enlightened*? What does *enlightened* mean?

The clues to *biological* are *body, give birth, provide milk*. These are all things that have to do with the body. In this context, *biological* means *pertaining to the body*.

SALLY FORTH By Greg Howard

Reprinted with speicial permission of NAS, Inc.

A woman's choice?

Ms. Gage says the decision to choose between work and family is one a woman must face "alone." What reason does she give for this opinion? Do you agree? Why or why not?

Do you believe mothers can do a good job at both work and family? Why or why not?

The sentences below come from viewpoints 1 and 2. Try to define each highlighted word by considering its use in context. You will find four possible definitions of the highlighted word under each sentence. Choose the definition that is closest to your understanding of the word. Use the dictionary to see how well you understood the words in context.

1. Still, "I wanted to do some things the way my mother used to," she says. She would rush home from work to **recreate** the home of her youth.

   a. make things better than they ever were before

   b. forget

   c. do things the way they used to be done

   d. destroy

2. While the issue of work and family will affect large companies and the government, women are not waiting for **corporations** or the government to act.

   a. clubs

   b. large companies

   c. schools

   d. the government

3. "Neither of us had loving parents, so we don't have many **parental** feelings," she says.

   a. like a parent

   b. secret

   c. not very important

   d. like a child

4. I am married to a wise man. He is **enlightened**.

   a. quiet

   b. friendly

   c. wise

   d. angry

CHAPTER

PREFACE: Do Children Benefit from Working Mothers?

A large number of women have been working outside the home for many years. This has given researchers time to study children who are raised by working mothers. How well do these children do in school? Do they seem happy? Do they get the attention they need?

People disagree over what this research proves about children whose mothers work. Some people see evidence that children of working mothers set higher goals for themselves. These children also seem to have greater self-esteem. Others disagree. They say that for children to learn important values, they need the constant attention of their own parents.

The authors of the following viewpoints debate whether having a mother who works helps children or harms them.

As you read, watch for highlighted words. Try to figure out their meanings from their use in context.

Children benefit from working mothers

Editor's Note: This viewpoint is paraphrased from a book by Anita Shreve. Ms. Shreve is a former editor and writer for *Us, Newsweek, New York,* and *Redbook* magazines.

One afternoon, I noticed my three-year-old daugher, Katherine, playing in the hallway. She sat at a small table, cutting up pieces of paper and pasting them onto larger sheets. She had a phone nearby, and a *Speak and Spell* game. She pretended this was a "computer." Occasionally, she paused to "write" on her papers.

"What are you doing?" I asked.

She looked up. "I can't talk to you right now," she said. "I have a lot of hard working to do. I have to write an article, I am going to have important phone calls, and you can't talk to me while I'm having them."

Except for a few changes, she had it right. The words were my words. The work was my work. Just as I had done many times, she was writing an article. She was announcing that she could not be disturbed. What interested me was not that she imitated me. All children **ape** their parents—pretending to shave in front of a mirror or to scold their dolls. What I found interesting was that she pretended to have a job. "Mommy works. If I want to be like Mommy, I work, too," she seemed to be saying.

What word is a clue to the meaning of *ape*? What does *ape* mean in this sentence?

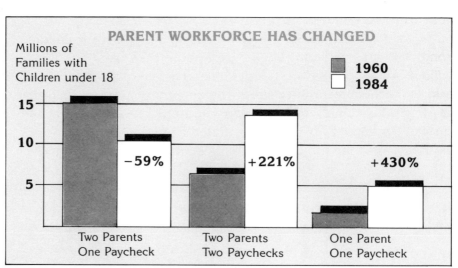

PARENT WORKFORCE HAS CHANGED

Millions of Families with Children under 18

■ 1960
□ 1984

15
10
5

−59%   +221%   +430%

Two Parents One Paycheck   Two Parents Two Paychecks   One Parent One Paycheck

SOURCE: Bureau of Labor Statistics and the Work and Family Information Center at the Conference Board

Mothers have always known they were "**role models**." For centuries, people have known that the example a mother sets shapes her child's behavior, beliefs, and values. In the past, girls were prepared for **nurturing** roles, such as taking care of children and supporting their husbands. Boys were prepared for active roles outside the home, such as earning a living. Today, this division of labor is changing. Mothers and fathers are preparing children of both sexes for work and for parenting.

Critics of the working mother suggest that she becomes a less important role model as the time she spends at home lessens. They ask whether a mother who spends only a few hours a day with her child can be as strong a role model as the at-home mother since the at-home mother is with the child all day.

Other researchers question whether measuring the total number of hours a mother spends with her child is the best way of judging the mother's strength as a role model. Lois Hoffman has found that working mothers spend less time with their children. However, she also found the time spent with them is more likely to be in direct contact with them.

Sandra Scarr, in her book *Mother Care, Other Care,* found that "the child of a mother at home full-time spends only 5 percent of her waking hours in direct **interaction** with her mother." She added that employed mothers spend as much time in direct contact with their children as mothers who stay home do. Working mothers spend the same number of hours reading to, playing with, and otherwise paying attention to their children. They do not, of course, spend as much time simply in the same room or house with the children.

The amount of time working mothers spend with their children strongly affects how many women feel about their work. A *Redbook* survey of one thousand women revealed that many working mothers feel guilty about the amount of time they spend away from their children. Many working mothers feel they are "missing something" by being separated from their children for long hours. But the majority felt that "quality time" with their

What ideas are a clue to the meaning of *role models*? What does *role models* mean?

What phrase is a clue to the meaning of *nurturing*? What does *nurturing* mean?

Look for clues to the meaning of *interaction* in the ideas surrounding it. What does *interaction* mean?

'Young man, your mother and I are giving you quality time, but you're not giving us quality time.'

children made up for the time they were absent. I'm not sure "quality time" is a good term. It suggests that a mother must "do something" with the child whenever they are together. I know from my own experience that I like being in the same room with my child, even if I am cooking or paying bills. This sense of nurturing and comfort—of having a loving adult nearby to take care of you—is at least as important to a child as being read to or taught something.

But is the mother the only one who can provide those long hours of nurturing and comfort? My daughter is as comfortable with her father in the room, or her grandmother, or a neighbor she knows wells, as she is with me. In many other cultures around the world—the Kikuyu society in Kenya, Africa, for example—children learn early on that nurturing comes from a variety of female adults and older girl children. In that society, all adult females are responsible for all children.

You should be familiar with *nurturing*. You learned it earlier in this viewpoint. What does *nurturing* mean?

Parents in our culture are not comfortable with the idea that children can have many nurturers. Finding the kind of care they want for their children is difficult. As a result, many mothers feel guilty about working outside the home. These bad feelings can become more important than the good feelings the mother has about her career.

A mother who feels guilty about working cannot be an effective role model. But when the mother is comfortable with her role as a working mother, her children may see her as a super role model with **enhanced** powers. She is seen as having greater power than either a father or an at-home mother. She has power both inside and outside of the home. She is able to convey a great sense of self-esteem, fulfillment, and accomplishment to her children.

What words provide clues to the meaning of *enhanced*? What does *enhanced* mean?

Are working mothers good role models?

Ms. Shreve says that children benefit from working mothers. Name one of the benefits she describes.

According to Ms. Shreve, a mother who works is often the strongest role model in the family. Who are some of your role models? They do not have to be members of your family.

Children benefit from mothers who stay home

Editor's Note: This viewpoint is paraphrased from an essay by Linda Burton. Ms. Burton is one of the founders of Mothers At Home, an organization for women who choose not to work outside their homes.

When I was twenty-two, I saw a woman in the parking lot of a supermarket who represented everything I never wanted to be. She was driving a station wagon and was yelling at her three children, who had ice cream dripping all over themselves. Groceries were spilling out of bags onto the back seat and floor. The woman's hair was uncombed. Her clothes looked as if she had slept in them. "Ugh," I said, pointing her out to a friend. "I will never let *that* happen to me!"

Feiffer

I told my friend that this woman would be a lot happier if she worked in an office. Her children drove her crazy. She did not enjoy being with them, probably because she was bored. What she needed was more mental excitement, work that **stimulated** her mind. What her children needed was a calm, loving mother. There was no question in my mind that she should get an interesting job and leave her kids with a sitter.

What word provides a clue to *stimulated*? What does *stimulated* mean?

I forgot about this incident until recently. I was in my car—a station wagon. I had not had much sleep because one of my children had been sick all night. I was in a hurry to buy some medicine at the drug store, so I had just thrown on some pants and a T-shirt. I had ignored my hair, hoping I could just "shake" it into shape on the way. I was thinking about a class I had to teach that night.

As I waited at a traffic signal, my eighteen-month-old son threw his bottle on the floor. The top came loose, and juice spilled out. He screamed for me to pick up the bottle. My three-year-old began to whine, so his brother screamed louder. The light turned green.

I had lost my patience. I pulled over to the side of the road and **upbraided** my children in a very unpleasant way. When I had finished scolding them, I settled back into my seat. Then I noticed a woman—about twenty-two—sitting in her car at the traffic light. She was staring at me in horror and disgust. Our eyes met for only an instant, but it was a moment of great insight.

What word is a clue to the meaning of *upbraided*? What does *upbraided* mean?

I had become the woman I never wanted to be. I was a living example of everything that could go wrong with motherhood. I thought for a moment that maybe I should get a job and let a more **tolerant** person take care of my children. They deserved to be with someone who would not get upset so easily. But for the time being, we were stuck with each other in a very small place. We could not walk away from the problem. I wanted to make things better, so I apologized.

What phrase is a clue to the meaning of *tolerant*? What does *tolerant* mean?

I told my children that I was sorry I had yelled. I admitted that it had not been fair, it had not been right, and I should not have done it. Then I asked if they knew why I had yelled.

My three-year-old nodded his head. "You were mad," he said.

I told him that I was not mad at him. "I am not really sure I was mad at all," I said. "I was tired, and sometimes being tired makes you feel mad. Isn't that silly?"

We discussed what had happened for a while longer, and we all seemed to feel much better as we continued our drive to the store.

That is when I made a firm decision to remain at home with my children. I knew no one could have taught them as much as I had in that car. I also knew there was no job that could teach me as much as I had learned during that one incident.

What had they learned? First of all, they learned that it is okay to be mad. Second, they learned that when we fail to do the right thing, there is usually something we can do about it—like apologize. Finally, they learned that sometimes when we feel angry, something else may really be going on, such as lack of sleep.

From this very bad time, I learned why it is important for me to be at home with my children. My goal is to teach them how to live successfully, how to get through life as well and as happily as possible. So much of our success in life, after all, is measured by how well we handle its difficulties. Many times, we are tired, frightened, or disappointed. If parents are not around to serve as examples for how to face **adversity**, how will their children learn the lessons?

One of the greatest joys of motherhood is watching our children become independent of us. But there are different ways to teach a child to become **autonomous**. One way is to spend less time with the child, and look after him or her less. This promotes one kind of independence, but is it the best kind? Have children gained autonomy because they have been ignored? Or have they gained autonomy because they have been supported while learning to do things for themselves? Do children know they can make it on their own because they are rich in skills and knowledge or because they have had to face much of life alone? Will they help others because they were helped along the way? Or will they ignore others because no one was ever there for them?

In their quiet moments of **reckoning**—summing up about the value of staying home—mothers must decide what is truly best for their children.

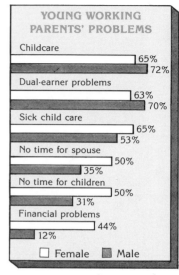

YOUNG WORKING PARENTS' PROBLEMS

Childcare — 65% / 72%
Dual-earner problems — 63% / 70%
Sick child care — 65% / 53%
No time for spouse — 50% / 35%
No time for children — 50% / 31%
Financial problems — 44% / 12%

☐ Female ▨ Male

SOURCE: Work and Family Resources, Afton, Minn.

What ideas are a clue to the meaning of *adversity*? What does *adversity* mean?

What word is a clue to the meaning of *autonomous*? What does *autonomous* mean?

What words are clues to the meaning of *reckoning*? What does *reckoning* mean?

Do children benefit from mothers who stay home?

What incident made Ms. Burton decide to stay home with her children? Do you think the author made the right decision? Why or why not?

Below are sentences with missing words. Choose words from the list at the left that best complete the sentences. You should be able to identify the appropriate word from its use in context.

autonomous
reckoning
tolerant
nurture
adversity
interact
stimulation
upbraid

1. Anita Shreve believes a parent can _____ a child by simply being in the same room with him or her, providing care and comfort without saying or doing anything special.

2. Sometimes parents think about how well they are raising their children. In these moments of _____, parents consider how much their children are learning, whether they seem happy, and how they get along with other kids.

3. Some people have jobs that excite their minds. Other people look outside of work for most of their mental _____.

4. Parents who encourage independence help their children become _____. Their children learn to do things for themselves and make more of their own decisions.

5. When parents are angry, they sometimes _____ their children. Some children respond to yelling with better behavior, some respond by acting worse.

6. Many parents try to teach their children how to handle _____. They believe that children who can cope with difficulties will be prepared to succeed as adults.

7. Many working parents believe that the people who care for their children full-time are more _____ than they could ever be. These parents admire the patience and understanding of their day-care providers.

8. Children in day care learn to _____ with large numbers of children. This talking, playing, and even fighting is an important part of growing up.

CHAPTER

PREFACE: **Does Day Care Help Children?**

Many working parents hire people outside the family to take care of their children during the day. The caregiver may come to the child's home, but usually the child goes to the caregiver's home. Many children go to a center specially designed to care for a number of children. This service is known as "day care."

Frequently, parents feel guilty about putting their children in day care. Many parents today were raised at home, and they worry that day care might be bad for their children. They are afraid their children might not do well in school. They fear their children will not learn important values, like honesty and patience.

Many people believe there is nothing to worry about. They say day care helps children grow in a variety of ways. They claim that day-care children are more independent and confident than children raised at home. They argue that day-care children may even do better in school and get along better with other people.

The next two viewpoints discuss the effects of day care on children. Both viewpoints quote experts who have studied day-care children. These experts may use terms that are new to you. Try to figure out the meaning of new words from their use in context.

Editor's Note: This viewpoint is paraphrased from a book by JoAnn Miller and Susan Weissman. JoAnn Miller is a writer and editor who specializes in psychology, the study of human behavior. Susan Weissman has a master's degree in social work and founded the Park Center Preschools in New York City.

Psychology was defined in the editor's note before this viewpoint. What does *psychologist* mean?

From this context, what does *colleagues* mean?

You should be able to figure out the meaning of *reunion* from its use as the opposite of *separation*. What does *reunion* mean?

You should be familiar with *stimulation*. This word appeared in a previous viewpoint. What does it mean?

In the last fifteen years, researchers have begun to compare home-reared children with those raised in day care. They have tried to find out if being in day care harms a child's development.

Researchers have observed children in day-care homes and centers. They have questioned parents and caregivers. They have measured the children's development. Most of the research has shown that day care itself produced few if any harmful effects.

Psychologist Jerome Kagan and those with whom he works at Harvard University spent six years comparing day-care children and those raised at home. Kagan and his **colleagues** found no important differences in development between the two groups. "If the child comes from a stable family and the day care is of good quality, the child's development seems to be normal," Kagan concluded.

Many parents worry that day care may break down the bond that exists between themselves and their children. Researchers are also concerned about the breaking down of this bond. Many researchers believe this bond affects a person's feelings of security throughout his or her life.

Researchers often measure this bond by separating a mother and child. They record how the child reacts to this separation. They also note what kind of **reunion** the mother and child have. In the vast majority of such experiments, day-care children separate from and reunite with parents in the same way as home-reared ones do.

Researchers have also studied whether children prefer their parents or their caregivers for comfort and stimulation. Parents need not worry. The majority of day-care children prefer their parents.

Since day-care children interact with more people than home-reared children, researchers have wondered whether day care makes a difference in **social development**. Their studies indicate that it does. Day-care children of all ages get along better with their peers than do home-reared children. They meet new children more easily, and they cooperate better.

What does the author mean by *social development*?

Research has also shown that there is a negative side to the effects of day care. Some researchers find day-care children to be **boisterous**. They are noisier and more active than children raised at home. Researcher Alison Clarke-Stewart points out that these may seem to be "negative" behaviors, but they may really be signs of children who have learned how to get along in the social world.

What does *boisterous* mean?

One study found that boys who had been in day care before the age of five were better liked when they became teenagers. But most social differences between day-care children and home-reared children disappear after the early grades.

Day-care children also perform better in school than do children reared at home, according to Alison Clarke-Stewart. But this difference does not last long. By second grade, home-reared students perform as well in school as their day-care-reared classmates.

Day-care children show some differences from children raised at home. But the most important thing is that day care does not have a harmful effect on how children learn or perform in school.

Does day care help children?

Ms. Miller and Ms. Weissman believe day care helps children. Name two positive qualities that they say day-care children possess.

Editor's Note: This viewpoint is paraphrased from a book by Fredelle Maynard. Fredelle Maynard studied at the University of Toronto and received a doctorate degree from Radcliffe College in Cambridge, Massachusetts. She has written several books about raising children.

You learned the meaning of *social development* and *boisterous* in previous viewpoints. What do these words mean?

What does *aggressiveness* mean?

What word is a clue to the meaning of *hostile*? What does *hostile* mean?

Many researchers have pointed out that day-care children exhibit greater social development than children raised at home. But the social confidence they show also has a negative side. Day-care children tend to be self-confident in the extreme. They are less polite than children raised at home. They will be loud and boisterous if they choose. They are not very concerned about what adults think or want. Since they are used to being in groups, they are less capable of entertaining themselves.

The main problem that day-care children exhibit is greater **aggressiveness**. Day-care children are more likely to get what they want by hitting, kicking, punching, insulting, and taking things without permission. A recent report found that day-care children perform fifteen times as many aggressive acts as home-reared children.

These children continue their aggressiveness when they enter school. They are more **hostile** to teachers and peers. They are also more easily distracted. The Tavistock Institute studied eight day-care graduates of average or above average intelligence. The study found that only one student achieved average levels in reading, language, and ability to concentrate.

Parents like to believe that they have the last word in teaching values to their children. But this may not be the case. Questions about values come up all day, even when parents are not there. "Children do not make notes about their questions to bring up at a more convenient time," writes Rita Kramer in her book *In Defense of the Family*, "They ask whoever is there at the moment." Jerome Kagan of Harvard University agrees. "A day-care center that cares for children from their sixth month to their sixth year has more than eight thousand hours to teach them values, beliefs, and behaviors."

The child in day care lives in an **artificial** world. He or she does not face real-life choices. At home a child can have a snack or go outdoors when he or she pleases. At the day-care center, the schedule decides such things. At home, children must learn what can and cannot be done. The stove is hot, knives are sharp, glass will break. They must make important choices. At day care children's choices are all **trivial**: puzzles or paints? Apple or orange juice?

To date, the only research measuring the effect of day care on children beyond the pre-school years is an eleven-year study conducted by T. Moore in London. Moore compared children raised at home until they were five with those who had been in day care for an average of two years. When the children were six, the day-care children were more aggressive and less concerned about punishment than the children raised at home.

Compared with home-reared boys, teenage males with a history of day care were described as more likely to tell lies to get out of trouble. They disagreed with their parents about their choice of friends. They used their parents' possessions without permission and took "things they knew they shouldn't have."

Boys raised in their own families could be trusted not to do things they should not do. Compared to the children who had received day care, they were more interested in school. They liked "making things" and showed "creative skills." They also read better and were more likely to remain in school.

According to Dr. Annette Silbert, a Boston psychologist, the real question is not whether day care or home care is better. The real question is, "What does it take to live in our society?" Silbert says that if we want our children to become adults who cooperate and who can adapt to change, then there are certain things we must do while caring for these children when they are young." Only the family can provide children with the basis of trust—in other people and in themselves—that they need.

What does *artificial* mean?

What does *trivial* mean?

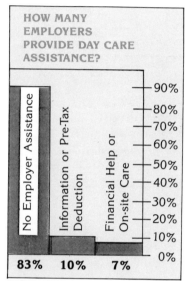

HOW MANY EMPLOYERS PROVIDE DAY CARE ASSISTANCE?

No Employer Assistance — 83%
Information or Pre-Tax Deduction — 10%
Financial Help or On-site Care — 7%

SOURCE: NCJW Center for the Child

Psychologist appeared in the previous viewpoint. What does it mean?

Does day care harm children?

Ms. Maynard believes day care harms children. What reasons does she give for this? Do you agree or disagree?

Understanding Words in Cartoons

Cartoonists use pictures to make us laugh, but they also use words. Most of the words cartoonists use are easy to understand. They want as many people as possible to enjoy their humor. But sometimes cartoonists use words that may be unfamiliar.

The cartoon below shows two young girls talking about their working mother. The children speak in language that could be used by a psychologist—it's not the way young girls would normally speak. By looking at the girls' language in context, however, you should be able to determine the meaning of the words.

profound
neurosis
charade
insecure
deterioration
conflicts
eating disorder
intimate

At the left is a list of words you may be unfamiliar with that are used in this cartoon.

Read the title of the cartoon and the cartoon. Pay close attention to the words listed for you above. First try to understand the unfamiliar words from the context in which they are used. Next, use a dictionary to look up any of the meanings you cannot figure out from the context. Finally, when you understand the words, answer the following questions:

Why do you think the cartoon is called "The Guilt that Drives Working Mothers Crazy?"

Name three things the girls claim will happen to them because their mother works.

Do you think the cartoonist thinks mothers *should* feel guilty about working? Why or why not?

After reading the cartoon, do you think working mothers help or harm their children? Why?